AVOIDING THE WASTEPAPER BASKET
A PRACTICAL GUIDE FOR APPLYING TO GRANT-MAKING TRUSTS

TIM COOK
Clerk of the City Parochial Foundation

Edited by Alan Dingle

Illustrations by Steve Simpson

London Voluntary Service Council
356 Holloway Road, London N7 6PA

British Library Cataloguing in Publication Data
A catalogue record for this book is available from the British Library

ISBN 1 872582 61 3
© London Voluntary Service Council 1996
Typeset in England by Boldface Typesetters, London
Printed by Russell Press, Nottingham

CONTENTS

Timothy Cook has worked for charities in London since 1962. Until 1985, when he joined the City Parochial Foundation and the Trust for London, he was regularly involved in making applications to trusts and other funding bodies. During his time at the Foundation he has read well over a thousand applications a year and visited some 400 projects a year. It is from this experience of both sides of the fence that this booklet has been written.

FOREWORD

It's always a pleasure to listen to Tim Cook. He takes risks, says the unpredictable in an unassuming way, and puts it all so clearly that the message gets through uncluttered by jargon.

This book is the same. Plenty of people advise voluntary organisations on how to raise funds. Some of them are LVSC's own staff. This is the first book I have known written by someone from a trust. Tim had worked in the voluntary sector all his life until he became Clerk to the Trustees of the City Parochial Foundation in 1986

He has used his experience to give us a practical and frank description of what it feels like to receive our applications. All his examples are true. I wish that I could refute them, and prove that voluntary agencies don't, for example, get funders' names wrong when we write to them. But apparently we do. I plan to review all my communications with our funders now I've read Tim's advice.

I hope that this book helps to build strong, honest and enduring relationships with funders. I can't think of a better person than Tim Cook to explain clearly, gently and with a smile, how to achieve this.

Christine Holloway
Director
London Voluntary Service Council

I

Introduction

In recent years, many directories, guidelines and booklets have been published and many seminars and courses held, all advising on how to apply to trusts and companies. Yet for some grant-givers, the overall standard of applications has not risen in response to all these fundraising aids. The reasons are not hard to see. Indeed, they are eminently understandable: overworked staff and committees; the lack of truly localised and specific advice; misleading directories; too many applicants chasing too little money. There is therefore little value in 'blaming' applicants or producing yet another blueprint. What, as a grant-giver, I have tried to do is to illustrate by actual (though anonymous) examples some of the worst and best features of the fairly typical applications that land on my desk daily and in quantity – some 10,000 of them over the last ten years.

This booklet will *not* tell you where to apply. The aim is to look at all the practical matters that need to be considered if an application is to avoid annoying the recipient, starting from the initial discussion about applying for funding. Trust staff are human too, and anything you can do to reduce their frustration and exasperation can only help the initial consideration of your application.

Let me also say that this is not a 'holier than thou' publication. When I joined the City Parochial Foundation in 1985, I looked up an application I submitted to it in 1967 that was still on the files. It was truly dreadful. I have learned since then. This guide is a personal attempt to share that learning.

GOOD APPLICATIONS HAVE ALWAYS BEEN POSSIBLE

In March 1893 the City Parochial Foundation received the following application written in a copperplate hand (no word-processors then and precious few trusts to write to!). It is certainly a model application.

'Sir

As Treasurer and Honorary Secretary of the Homes for Working Boys in London, I write to ask you to be good enough to bring before the Central Governing Body at an early meeting the question of providing lodgings for lads engaged in Warehouses, Offices, and Workshops in the City and other parts of the Metropolis, and to suggest that no more suitable object could be found for the funds administered by the Central Governing Body.

In old times apprentices and lads engaged in the City found a home in their master's house over the workshop, but now it is hardly possible for employers to provide sleeping accommodation. At any rate it is very seldom done.

The number of boys engaged in the City who have no home of their own has no doubt greatly increased and in many cases boys are compelled by the high rents of rooms to resort to common lodging houses or at any rate to obtain a share of a bed in some small room where the surroundings are most injurious to health and morals.

A great deal has been done of late years by Industrial Dwellings Companies and Trusts to provide dwellings for the Working Classes, and lately, model lodging houses have been erected which will no doubt be a great boon to those for whom they are intended, but homeless working boys derive no benefit from these buildings.

The Polytechnics and other similar Institutions provide education and recreation, but are of little practical use to those whose first requirement is a home.

The Society which I represent has accommodation for 380 boys in their eight Homes, one of which is within the City and four others are within ten minutes walk of it.

The boys admitted are all at work, and they all pay for their food and something for their lodging. The only qualification for admission is that they can work and that they have no home of their own. Some come from Orphanages and Industrial Schools while others apply of their own accord having seen notices of the Homes in the Post Offices or in Lockhart's Cocoa Rooms.

It is needless to say that the Homes are not self-supporting. If elder boys who are earning good wages were only admitted their Contributions would be almost sufficient, but the Committee are most anxious to help those who are able to earn only 5/-s to 7/-s per week. In addition to the boys' payments the Committee requires every year about £3,000 of which £1,200 is in annual subscriptions.

The Committee have lately been obliged to rebuild their principal Home which is in Spital Square just outside the City boundary in the parish of Norton Folgate. They have received over £4,500 for this purpose, but require another £2,000 to complete.

The Building is held on a lease of 99 years but the Committee have the option of purchasing the freehold for a sum of £3,500, by which they will be relieved of an annual rent of £140.

I have always felt that the maintenance of this City Home for Working Boys was an

This was not at all untypical of the applications made to the Foundation more than a hundred years ago.

A not untypical application of today, which leaves much to be desired, is:

HOW DOES THIS HAPPEN?

How can a charity desperately in need of funds send off one or even dozens of applications along the lines of the above? It is certainly done with the best of intentions, but is highly unlikely to fire the enthusiasm of funders.

<h1 style="text-align:center">II</h1>

The treasure hunt begins

When things go wrong with an application, the reasons often lie in how the decision to apply was made.

WHO MADE THE DECISION?

Did the whole committee or just the chair decide to raise funds either generally or by applying to a few trusts for a specific grant? It is better if at least a few of the committee can be involved in the decision.

Did the director just apply and then tell the chair? Did the project worker just apply and then tell the director?

WHY WAS THE DECISION MADE?

Was the decision a result of considered discussion by the committee – or was it made in haste when the Treasurer revealed the anticipated deficit for next year or, even worse, the deficit for this year?

HOW WERE THE TRUSTS CHOSEN?

Was the decision made to apply to the 'Cook Trust' because someone had heard they had funds available for counselling – even though counselling is not something the applicant charity actually does!

Who is delegated to find out about trusts and write to them? Is it the overworked director, an absent committee member who 'knows people in the trust world', a less-than-enthusiastic chairperson, a volunteer fund-raiser or a student on placement?

One very hot summer's day I visited a project in East London to discuss their application to the Foundation. They were pleased to see me, as they had sent out 800 applications to trusts and I was the first sign of life. I advised them to send no more applications, as their indiscriminate, scatter-gun approach was highly unlikely to generate the large sum they needed. They told me they had a volunteer working his way through a directory – he was now at T and wanted to get to the end of the alphabet. It was hard to know how to respond charitably and constructively.

Taking the time to identify a few appropriate trusts and target them is more likely to succeed than writing to a hundred, let alone 800. The larger the sums of money you need, the more important targeting becomes.

WHO SUPERVISES THE PROCESS?

Whoever is sending off the applications, someone needs to supervise the process. When I receive two applications from the same charity in the same week from two different people and for totally different purposes, I do worry about supervision!

GETTING IT AS RIGHT AS POSSIBLE IS IMPORTANT

The answers to the above questions often provide a clue to the problems with the application. I understand how it can all go wrong: a committee meeting running late into the evening, a full agenda, a sense of panic about the finances, a desperate need to dash for cash and a general feeling that the director should 'do something'. But once a second-rate application is in the post, it is usually too late to put it right.

The written communication with the trust will usually be your only communication; there will be little chance of sending follow-up material to clarify what was obscure in the original.

What can be done to reduce the chances of putting that second-rate application into the post?

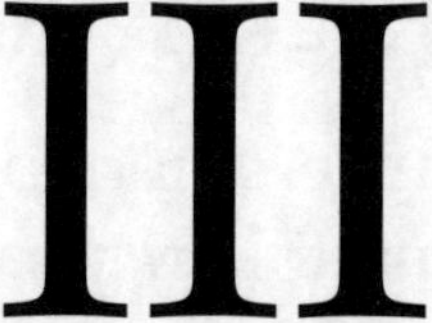

Details matter

If you seriously want £10,000, try to avoid…

> *'Dear Sir/Madam'*

or

> *'Ms Margaret Hyde*
> *Esmee Fairbairn Charitable Trust*
>
> *Dear Sir'*

or

> *'Timothy Cook*
> *Clerk to the Trustees*
>
> *Dear Mr Clarke'*

or

> *'Timothy Clerk*
> *Cook to the Trustees'*

Try to avoid writing to the City Parochial Foundation and then beginning your letter:

> *'We are extremely grateful to the support we have had in the past from the Tudor Trust and hope we might ask you again for a further grant.'*

Has the letter actually been signed? A surprising number of applications arrive unsigned and undated.

WHO FINALLY CHECKED THE APPLICATION?

The 1893 application set out earlier referred to a copy of the Report being enclosed; it was, and the copy is still on file. One recent application from a university stated :

> *'The enclosed documents outline the aims and purpose of such an exhibition, as well as giving details of estimated budgets and educational outreach programmes.'*

No documents at all were included. Do I ignore the letter, telephone, write a letter of request, or wait for the documents to arrive?

It is important that applications acknowledge any previous grants from the trust now being approached; sadly they often fail to do that.

For example, if a charity has had £10,000 a year for the last three years from the City Parochial Foundation and begins its letter

> *'I would like to introduce you to the work of the Youth Homelessness Project'*

it is truly hard to know how to respond civilly.

This is no better:

> *'I am aware we recently had a grant from the City Parochial Foundation which I believe has now finished, but I am afraid we have no records on our files. Could you send me photocopies of all the earlier correspondence so a new application can be prepared.'*

IV

Please try to be clear

An application which is hard to understand must have a reduced chance of success. This is not a question of the problems that can arise when English is a second language: that can easily be taken into account. Obscurity arises in a number of ways.

The letter is peppered with initials of organisations. You will know your own field of work very well – but you should assume the trust will not. I do not feel the slightest bit insulted if the names of organisations are given to me in full. A great deal of time can be wasted in trying to find out just what LASA, LVSC, LBGC, LABS, GLAAS and a thousand other sets of initials actually stand for.

Many applications fail to mention any sum of money at all, making an intelligible initial response much more difficult:

> *I am writing to you to enquire whether or not the City Parochial Foundation would consider providing capital funding for a tenants' community room on a housing association development.'*

The letter then describes the project, which includes the building of more than 60 houses, and concludes:

> *'I would appreciate if you would consider us for funding in the year 1995-96 or failing that 1997-98.'*

It is difficult to respond easily or satisfactorily to the following appeal:

> *'We felt that you would have ideas, strategies, information and a sense of vision which would contribute to the successful planning of this venture. We would welcome an opportunity to meet you, show you the proposals so far and hear your thoughts on the project.'*

Lack of clarity is unhelpful, particularly when no hard factual information is given about the service for which a grant is being sought, as a trust will not readily be able to understand why you need a grant.

> *'This very busy advice centre needs...'*
>
> *'The youth club is well attended on every evening...'*

Always give the actual number of people who attend or benefit from the organisation.

- Avoid 'a well-attended conference'; use instead 'a conference attended by 275 people'.

- Avoid 'much valued by the local community'; use instead

> *'47 people attended once/twice per week over the 48 weeks that we were open in the last year'.*

- Avoid 'we had an excellent outing to the seaside'; use instead

> *'we arranged a trip to Brighton for 27 pensioners, and three grandchildren came too – photograph attached'.*

V

Leaving the trust to do the work

However busy you are, the trust staff are unlikely to be any less busy – and remember that you want something from them rather than vice versa. It is therefore ill-advised to expect the trust to do your work for you. This happens often, and in quite odd ways.

- Applicants can seem to throw themselves on the trust's mercy and leave it to do all the work:

'As we fall within your remit, I wonder if there would be any form of help available, in the form of sponsorship perhaps, or grant aid, sponsoring a production or help of a practical kind.'

'Whilst on a fund-raising course recently, I was fortunate enough to meet staff from the CVS, and they suggested I write to you with a view to obtaining a grant for our association.

The attached literature will I feel sure assist you in reaching a decision on this matter.'

- Those who anticipate a negative response often ask for a lead to someone else, thus placing the trust staff in the inappropriate role of quasi-fund-raisers:

'We have been told that you may be able to help us with funding or even that you may be able to let us know of another organisation that could help us.'

- The application is a brief letter attached to a series of documents, each referred to in the letter as providing information necessary to the application. One recent application consisted of a four-line letter and seven documents:

- A common method of shifting the burden on to the trust is to submit a shopping list of needs and ask for advice on which is most appealing to the trustees, so that the application most likely to succeed can be developed. It is like telling the bookmaker you rather like five horses and could he advise on the one likely to win so you can place your bet with greater optimism. When trust staff are having to consider hundreds of applications, it is unhelpful to have even one applicant hedging his or her bets with a catalogue of needs. If it has to be done – and sometimes it may be necessary – then a phone call is a better way to do it.

VI

Emotional appeals

Tugging at the heartstrings does not take your application to the top of anyone's pile. Trusts do not have a league table of deserving causes. Applications have to be carefully assessed, not rated according to the teardrops generated in the recipient.

> *'Unless the Charity can raise some help with funding urgently, we may well close down. We need £35,000 to pay our rent and other expenses by the end of the year.*
>
> *I don't expect you to send us £35,000 but a generous donation would be "just in time".'*

or

> *'Dear Mr Cook*
>
> *I am asking for two minutes of your time.*
>
> *Our initial experimental funds are about to run out and our phone will stop ringing, unless you can help to keep us going.*
>
> *Will you answer this call with a cheque?'*

A powerful kind of appeal is the 'urgent' or 'emergency' application. Trusts on the whole do not respond readily to such appeals. Assessment is more difficult in such circumstances, and timetables often make it impossible. But even more important, as far as the City Parochial Foundation is concerned, is that whenever I have been persuaded to cut corners on an emergency application, the money granted has *never* been claimed with anything remotely like the urgency so graphically described in the original application.

A subtler form of emotive appeal (and applicants do try!) is one which appeals to the trust officer's good nature and intelligence.

> 'This is a proven and cost-effective operation which deserves your Trustees' generous support. Accordingly, I invite them to make a grant in the sum of £5,000. (Cheques should be made out to…and sent to me at the above address.)'

They should be so lucky.

VII

Length

The question most often asked is: 'How long should an application be?' It is simple to answer: two sides of A4. But, says the applicant, 'it is not possible to describe our work in such a short space'. So in comes the application with the comment: 'I know you asked me to restrict it to two pages, but I hope you will forgive the 20 pages enclosed.'

A good proposal can be made in two, or at the very most three, sides of A4. The longer the application, the greater the danger that the focus of the work will become unclear and the thinking behind the proposal less disciplined. My longest history essays at school rarely gained me my best marks. Exciting applications do come in short, sharp packages.

VIII

Guidelines

Many trusts now publish guidelines on what they will or will not consider funding. Directories give important details about an enormous number of trusts. If available, obtain some up-to-date guidelines before writing to a particular trust. Once you have received the printed information, read it from start to finish – and believe what it says. Certain mistakes are always cropping up:

- Failing to read the section that carefully lists what will not be funded.

- Assuming that the deadline for completion of applications is just a rough guide rather than a statement of fact.

- Going to inordinate lengths to justify why your charity really *does* fit the priorities, rather than acknowledging the reality of the text.

- Only paying attention to one part of the guidelines – for example, ignoring information about the time it will take to consider an application because of the need for a member of staff to visit – and instead seizing on a particular deadline and sending the application by courier or fax on that date, having made no previous contact at all

- Writing *'I am sorry, I didn't read the whole of the guidelines'* – this will not be greeted with enthusiasm.

If you do not read and absorb the available guidelines, it is likely that you will make assumptions about what the trust will or will not fund. An applicant may, for example, apply for a small capital grant. A visit is made, and it soon becomes clear in discussion that what is needed is an administrator's salary. When the applicant is asked why he or she did not apply for that, the answer often given is, *'Oh, I didn't know you made revenue grants.'* That kind of assumption arises daily. But not all trusts are able to visit and discuss applications, so the correspondence will be taken at face value and a golden opportunity may be missed.

The perfect illustration of this was the letter I received in February 1989 from a community centre. In it they described a thriving centre and asked the Foundation to fund three capital items: a second-hand piano for £1,000, a new bingo machine for £313.95 and a carpet for the under-fives room costing £350.

I visited the centre, to find it every bit as thriving as described. What was needed most of all was a childcare coordinator, which they had assumed, for no apparent reason, we would not fund. The eventual application in November 1989 secured a grant of £42,000 over three years for the post. A further £27,000 for the same post was given in 1992 and another grant in 1996. The initial visit also led to discussions about plans for the building. I suggested a trust to apply to and a six-figure grant resulted. And it all began with a piano…

IX

Phrases to avoid

Charities exist to meet many sorts of need. Trusts exist to help meet those needs – though not all trusts are interested in all of them. Applications are a means of communicating what a charity does and what in particular it requires money for. Trying too hard to impress the trust is not helpful, especially when everyone else is doing the same: if all the candidates in the history exam use the same quotations about Napoleon, no one gains any credit.

Worrying terms that occur include:

'Unique'. How do you know? When did you last visit voluntary organisations in, say, Grimsby?

'We work in the most deprived area of London/England/the United Kingdom'. The evidence is rarely cited – and besides, the fact that a charity works in such an area says nothing about the quality of its work.

'You will, I am sure, be familiar with the problems of homelessness.' Leaving aside the rather ambiguous nature of this statement, it is a lazy way of presentation as it avoids any basic statement of evidence.

'Two of your trustees are well-known to our Chairman.' Do I run for cover?

'Any help you can give us, however small, will be appreciated.' Would £100 from a trust giving out £5 million a year really be appreciated?

'A video showing our work much better than I can describe it is enclosed.' Does the trust have a video recorder, and does the trust director know how to work it?!

X

The final stage

When you think the application is complete and ready to post, ask someone unfamiliar with your work to read it and comment critically on it. That person may be the best surrogate trust director you will have. You believe in your charity and work hard for it and cannot take a detached view. You are not always aware which are the most interesting and positive aspects of your work. How often people have said to me, *'Oh, I didn't think that was of interest to you,'* or *'We just take that for granted – we had no idea it was such a different way of running an advice service.'*

Do try to obtain an outside view before the envelope, and possibly your fate, is sealed.

Remember that you are in effect entering a competition. Think how you would respond when advertising a vacancy if the job applicants sent in badly worded CVs and missed the advertised closing date.

Once your application has been sent to a trust, keep the trust informed of any significant changes: success with other funders, the resignation of the director, the termination of the lease on your premises – to name but a few of the typical events that have not been communicated to me when I was processing an application.

XI

Getting it right

Applications which land on the desk and set matters out clearly are not common but are by no means rare. Both large and small organisations produce them, and the applicant's first language does not have to be English. Most fundraisers do not naturally hit the right tone. The final pages of this booklet give examples of applications that got it as right as can reasonably be expected.

No approach can guarantee a grant, but the effort involved (on both sides) in unravelling a poor application is enormous. Time spent on the first application is time well spent.

XII

The application is successful

If your application is successful, you should not jeopardise the possibility of a continuing relationship with the trust. Many applicants do.

The Foundation sends a detailed letter offering grants and requesting acknowledgement within 14 days. At least ten per cent fail to meet that deadline. This is not a good start.

The Foundation asks for audited accounts and annual reports as part of the conditions of the grant. Again, a surprising number of applicants do not send them, and some have to be chased.

The staff member dealing with the funder leaves and the files are not handed on. The grant remains unclaimed, or is claimed after a year has gone by. In the latter case, it is reasonable to ask whether the money is really needed, as the costs have clearly been met during the year the grant was unclaimed.

The post-holder funded by the Foundation leaves but the first we hear of it is via an advertisement in the *Guardian*. This is tactless and to be avoided.

If serious problems develop in your organisation, inform the trust. It is better to do that than let it hear the rumours at second or third hand.

If you acknowledge a trust's grant in your annual report, pay attention to detail. It is irritating to have the City Parochial Foundation thanked as the London Parochial Trust.

XIII

DO

- Be sure you know why you are applying to the particular trust
- Read carefully any available guidelines
- Check the trust's name and address
- Check that the name of trust contacted corresponds with the trust named in the letter itself
- Check you are within the trust's priorities and area of benefit
- Sign the letter
- Ensure your organisation has a system for knowing who has written to which trusts
- Make sure that all necessary documents are enclosed
- Keep the basic application to two sides of A4
- Meet the deadline given
- Make the application specific, including a stated sum of money required
- Be specific about your activities and who uses them
- Ask someone outside the organisation to read through your application
- Have a clear organisational policy on writing to trusts
- If in doubt, check with the trust by phone before sending off an application

DON'T

- **Make emotional appeals**
- **Ask vaguely for assistance**
- **Present shopping lists of needs**
- **Write a brief letter referring to lots of other papers**
- **Use initials of organisations**
- **Lose the files referring to the application**
- **Write over-long applications and then apologise**

- *Don't invite the wastepaper basket*

EXAMPLE
A

Application from the British Association of Settlements and Social Action Centres (BASSAC)

Total sum required: £6,878 in each of three years
£20,634 in all

WHAT IS BASSAC AND WHAT DOES IT DO?

1. BASSAC was founded in 1920 and is a network of 65 social centres, all of them in urban areas based on the original University Settlements but including many more recent inner-city community resource centres. There are 43 BASSAC centres in London spread across 14 Inner London boroughs. BASSAC is their support agency. Between them they have over 600 pieces of work and support over 1,000 other local groups.

2. BASSAC itself employs the equivalent of 3.8 staff. It provides information, advice, training and management support to its members. Its core costs are provided by the Voluntary Services Unit at the Home Office, the London Boroughs Grants Unit, and the Department of Health (in the form of a fee for administering £270,000 Opportunities for Volunteering funds). These grants total £92,000. The members pay affiliation fees which in the last year totalled just over £14,000. All other project costs (in the last year over £30,000) have to be raised through trusts, company donations etc.

3. In a recent review of its work conducted for the Home Office the consultant said of BASSAC 'Its grant is not large but the services provided are of high quality (as recorded by the membership and observed by the reviewer). In so far as it is possible to judge value for money I would argue that BASSAC gives it.'

THE PAN-LONDON COMMUNITY REGENERATION PARTNERSHIP

4. BASSAC has been encouraged by the Government Office for London to submit a bid to the Single Regeneration Challenge Fund for funding over seven years. The aim of the partnership is to build the capacity of local community groups across London so that they can participate in and benefit from major regeneration schemes in their neighbourhoods. The scheme is essentially a brokerage agency. A pool of money and a pool of trainers skilled in regeneration processes will be established. Tailored training and consultancy can then be provided to community groups in response to their own perceived needs.

5. The Partners are BASSAC, London Voluntary Service Council, African Caribbean Community Development Unit, Business in the Community, The Civic Trust, Community Development Foundation, Development Trusts Association, Federation of Independent Advice Centres, Community Links, London Regional Network of the Urban Forum, Project Fullemploy, British Telecom and two London Training and Enterprise Councils (CENTEC and LETEC).

6. The principle of SRB funding is that it expects to unlock other money from private and voluntary sector partners. In-kind commitments already amount to £104,000 to match a figure from SRB of £125,000. Applications to charitable trusts amount to a further £50,000.

7. If successful the programme will be managed by BASSAC for its first three years. John Matthews is one of the key figures in the voluntary sector response to urban policy and community regeneration. He has helped to found the National Urban Forum and was its Chair until recently. He has led this current bid, and BASSAC's work in local areas provides a major resource for the success of the scheme.

   This application is for CPF to pay BASSAC the equivalent of one day a week of John Matthews' time and costs to free him to manage the programme.

HOW WILL THIS BENEFIT THE POOR INHABITANTS OF LONDON?

8. At present major regeneration schemes are being agreed without local people being given any long-term role in helping to shape the schemes. Their neighbourhoods are subject to upheaval and physical change without their participation and too often physical regeneration is not matched by social and community regeneration. This programme will

give local people the training and skills they need to participate. It will make sure that they benefit from the regeneration of their neighbourhood, that they can help deliver significant parts of regeneration schemes themselves and that they can be full members of regeneration partnerships including sitting on the Board.

9. The programme has four planks:

- information and initial training about how to enter partnerships
- developmental training at the stage of planning and bidding
- training for key individuals to equip them to be Directors in partnerships
- training in financial management and control of assets that will be transferred to local communities as part of regeneration schemes.

Over the course of the programme 1680 groups will have been assisted. There are 30% targets for black and minority ethnic involvement at each stage.

THE COST

This has been calculated at 20% of the salary and on-costs

Salary:	£5085
Pension and N.I.	£1168
Office support	£625
Total each year	£6878
Total over 3 years	£20634

1995

EXAMPLE
B

Dear Mr Cook

We write to ask the City Parochial Foundation to support this association
in establishing a New Technology Training Centre for women in Newham
by funding the Centre's creche.

WHO WE ARE

We are a registered charity committed to the provision and promotion of
access to education and training opportunities for local women who, for a
variety of reasons, have been denied such facilities.

At the moment we have three full-time workers and four sessional creche
workers who, through the Co-ordinator, are responsible to a management
committee elected annually from the membership of the association. This
is made up of ex-trainees of the project, local councillors and affiliated
groups and individuals who live or work in the borough.

WHAT WE DO

Since 1984, the Women's Employment Project has run three Return to
Work Courses for women each year. These provide 'tasters' in a wide variety of manual trades, computing, literacy, numeracy and confidence building skills for women who have been out of work or under-using their skills
or potential. Sixty-three percent of former trainees have gone on to further
education or training or have found work in various manual trades, computing or general office work. The range of further education taken runs
from GCSE through Access to Higher Education and Social Work to
degrees at the London School of Economics and technical training at

Vauxhall College and Tower Hamlets Advanced Technology Training Centre.

The project's other activities include women's studies courses, workshops on food and alcohol and understanding health and hygiene. With Newham Community College we pioneered a Black Haircare Course which has now become part of mainstream college provision and will shortly have City & Guilds certification.

THE NEW TECHNOLOGY TRAINING CENTRE

In the light of changing employment patterns and in order to meet the challenge of the new employment opportunities opening up in the Docklands area, we established a local need for training in new technology for women in Newham. This need was recognised by the European Commission who have awarded us a grant of £175,593 from the European Social Fund under their Innovatory Programme to set up such a centre. With the aid of this funding and match-funding from the Department of the Environment under the Inner Area Programme, we will be able to move to larger premises in the centre of Stratford which will be fully accessible to women with disabilities.

We will be able to offer one-year full-time certificated courses, with training allowances, to twenty women a year in computing, microprocessing, robotics and electronic servicing. This will be in addition to our existing programme.

On these courses, priority will be given to women from local ethnic minority communities whose qualifications are not recognised in the UK, women with few or no formal education qualifications, the long-term unemployed and women wishing to retrain following childcare responsibilities. Forty per cent of the places we offer will be for women with disabilities.

THE CRECHE

The Association considers the provision of free childcare an essential requirement for a project which aims to attract all women regardless of their economic or personal circumstances. All our activities are therefore supported by free creche facilities for babies and pre-school children.

We also see creche provision as a positive benefit to children from areas of high deprivation, many of whom live in high rise flats (Newham has the highest rate of children under 5 living above the 5th floor of tower blocks in England) or bed and breakfast accommodation. They lack good facilities and many come from single parent families. We have a high proportion whose first language is not English and who have special needs as a result.

In our new premises (a former youth centre in Deanery Road, Stratford) we intend to convert the existing sports hall into a creche. Partitions need to be put in, the floor surface needs to be changed and the heating and lighting adapted and made safe. The creche will also need to be redecorated and new equipment purchased, as our present equipment is inadequate for increased size.

FUNDING FOR THE CRECHE

Although we have funding which will cover both our revenue costs and the capital expenditure necessary to convert an old youth centre into a fully equipped new technology training tentre with disabled access, none of our funding is specifically available for the creche. Funding under the Inner Area Programme is exclusively for revenue costs, and the policy of the Department of Employment is to exclude amounts for creche provision from the ESF bids they recommend to the European Commission.

We are therefore seeking an alternative source of funding for the creche. We would be very grateful if the City Parochial Foundation felt able to support this Project by funding the creche.

HOW MUCH WILL IT COST?

Our architects estimate that the necessary works to the creche will come to about £9,000. (The total works will be in the region of £104,000). I enclose a breakdown of their costs and their plans for the creche area. To benefit from the ESF grant we have to have our new courses started by the end of 1988. We hope to commence work on our new premises in late August/early September. So we are looking to receive funding for the creche during the current financial year.

I enclose a copy of our latest annual report to give you a clearer idea of our recent activities. We would be very happy for the Trustees, or their representatives, to visit the project and see our new premises. To arrange a visit,

or for any further information you need, please do not hesitate to contact
Marcene Hayden – our Acting Co-ordinator – at the address above.

I look forward to hearing from you.

Yours sincerely
Chair, Management Committee

1988

*The project has asked for it to be stated that their applications have since
improved. However, it remains an excellent application – and the original covered
only two sides of A4. (TC)*